DATING ESSENTIALS FOR MEN

KING OF HEARTS

Take The World of Dating By Storm

Frederico Lachlan

Table of Contents

PART 1 5
Chapter 1: 9 Ways Women Fall In Love 6
Chapter 2: 10 Signs You're In A Healthy Relationship 11
Chapter 3: 10 Signs Someone Has A Crush On You 18
Chapter 4: 10 Ways To Build A Strong Relationship 24
Chapter 5: 10 Signs You're Not Ready To Be In A Relationship 31
Chapter 6: 10 Signs You're Dating A Sociopath 37
Chapter 7: 10 Signs Your Crush Likes You 42
PART 2 49
Chapter 1: 10 Signs You're Falling In Love 50
Chapter 2: What To Do When Your Partner Cheats On You 56
Chapter 3: How To Survive A Long Distance Relationship 59
Chapter 4: What Happens When You Get Bored In A Relationship .. 65
Chapter 5: Feeling Insecure In Your Relationship 68
Chapter 6: Dealing With Money In Relationships 71
Chapter 7: How To Deal With Feeling Anxious In A Relationship 74
Chapter 8: Dealing With Abuse In A Relationship 76
PART 3 80
Chapter 1: 9 Tips On How To Have A Strong Relationship 81
9 Tips on How To Have A Strong Relationship 81
Chapter 2: 10 More Signs You Aren't Ready For A Relationship 88
Chapter 3: 9 Signs Of A Toxic Relationship 93
Chapter 4: 10 Ways Men Fall In Love 98
Chapter 5: 9 Signs an Introvert Likes You 105
Chapter 6: 8 Signs You Have Found Your Soulmate 110
Chapter 7: 8 Signs A Girl Likes You 115

PART 1

Chapter 1:
9 Ways Women Fall In Love

Opening

What makes a woman fall in love with men? Different TV shows and movies portray various scenarios of women falling in love only with rich and handsome guys. Think the Bachelor or some cheesy dating show. As a result we are incline to think that women will only like us if we are rich and handsome as well. But in reality women are far more complex and do see past the money, glamour, and attractive looks, to something that holds more dearly to their heart.

While women fall in love differently than men, they strongly desire their partners to respect, understand, love, and appreciate them for who they are. As a guy, it can be complicated to know the different ways that women fall in love with men. We make this easier for you. In this video, we will share eight different ways that they do just that. Let's get started!

1. She desires to be familiar with you

While this is true for both sexes, women show a greater desire to know their partner through spending quality time and making meaningful memories together. This helps them develop a more profound understanding of a potential soul mate. A woman wants to know if he is the one that she can build a memorable future together. On the contrary, men tend to favor the need to feel attraction in the beginning of a relationship, which I must say is usually mostly physical.

If she desires to be familiar with you, it is a sign that she might be considering you for the part. It is significant to remember that while physical looks are important, your personality and a deep personal and emotional connection is the one that will determine if a woman will fall in love with you.

2. They look for thoughtfulness

Being highly thoughtful themselves, women feel excited and much happier with a thoughtful man. They fancy feeling special, desired, and appreciated a top priority in an ideal partner that can give that to them. Receiving a sweet text message or flowers is extremely romantic for many women. They also truly admire men who remember special dates and occasions. If you can do these things with your eyes closed, you have already won half the battle.

3. She wants to know your Thoughts

Estrogen is known as the female sex hormone and it plays an integral role in remembering special memoirs, comprehending abstract conceptions, and other general webbed thoughts. A woman wants to know that her partner can initiate and understand meaningful or logical perceptions.

While it is wonderful to connect with someone through enjoyable dates and activities, women don't fall in love unless they are attracted to someone's thought-oriented personality. Do we appreciate similar life perspectives? Does he inspire me to advance my life knowledge? Intelligence is the most important aspect of a healthy relationship. A woman does not look for an intelligent partner to answer her questions, but she is particularly interested in discovering momentous life philosophies with her partner.

4. She desires to have a great communicator

Being able to have regular great conversations with a man is something highly sought after in women. Women often fall in love knowing they can engage in healthy communications with their partners. Having a meaningful connection is key here.

Do you know women particularly check the verbal communication skills of their partners to establish a deeper understanding of their personalities? It does not mean women don't appreciate silence, but a good balance between the two is the takeaway here. Women fall in love with guys who participate in good debates that challenge them intellectually without coming across as arrogant.

5. Value for Family

It's highly attractive for women to see a man giving higher consideration to his or her family. A woman truly appreciates a man who takes great care of his family and treats them with due respect. It is an obvious sign that he will give the same amount of respect to her as well. She feels truly grateful when he introduces her to his parents and exerts all his efforts to win the hearts of her family.

While we may not be able to control how family members think and behave, it is the effort and initiative of a man to win their approval that makes them the apple of any woman's eye.

6. She wants to have a trustworthy partner

While it may be controversial to say in this day and age, biologically, women are child-bearers. If having a child is a priority for a woman, they will naturally have a desire to find someone who is proven to be a reliable and trustworthy partner. A partner that will prioritize being a father some day and all that major responsibilities that come with it as a result. A woman will fall in love with a man knowing that they will be able to provide and take care of the family in the future.

If having kids is not a priority, having a trustworthy partner in other areas such as fidelity is also significant for a woman. Knowing she can trust you will be an easy way to win over her heart.

7. She desires to know if she can be herself with you

While it equally applies to both men and women, it does not lessen its significance when a woman determines it before falling in love. Since vulnerability is a widely accepted element in having sincere feelings for someone, a woman wishes to know if you can accept her for who she is without changing anything about her. A woman truly falls for a guy who accepts her the way she is and appreciates her presence in his life.

8. Please be gentle, man

Now last but not least...!

A woman will never give her sincere feelings to someone who is not gentle to her. Having a supportive, loving, caring, and easygoing partner is one of the top elements that women consider while falling in love.

Having a trustworthy and gentle partner to navigate through life's journey is the fundamental priority of every woman.

Closing

So that's it for today's video. What do you think about these ways of women falling in love? Do you know about any others? Let us know in the comments section below. Do not forget to subscribe to our channel, like, and share this video.

Thank you!

Chapter 2:
10 Signs You're In A Healthy Relationship

Good relationships are a prime ingredient for a happy life, and a bad one tends to be a miserable experience. We all know there's plenty of toxic relationships out there. We've seen them, and for many of us, we have been in them. According to a survey, a third of women and a quarter of men have experienced abusive relationships on average.

The term "perfect relationship" is nothing more than a myth. You don't just get one served on a plate. According to a therapist, "One thing healthy relationships largely share is adaptability. They adapt to circumstances because we can't escape the fact that we're always changing and going through different phases in life." It's not a secret that we all have our ups and downs and ebbs and flows, from time to time. And this may as well affect our relationship too. But one shouldn't strive for a perfect relationship; instead, endeavour to make the best one can.

Let's get to the heart of the matter: How do you know that you're in a healthy and robust relationship, or better stated: How do you know you're in a relationship that's good for you? These signs of a healthy relationship may be blazingly obvious, but sometimes we need things written in black and white for us to see that we're on the right path.

1. **You both understand the need for personal space:**

Healthy relationships are all about interdependence; that is, you rely on each other for mutual support but still maintain your identity as a unique individual. A famous saying goes, "Stand together, yet not too near together: For the pillars of the temple stand apart, And the oak tree and the cypress grow not in each other's shadow."
You don't wholly depend on your partner and know that you have a social circle outside of the relationship. Although you're always there for each other, you don't cling to your partner for every little need, and you spend your time pursuing your interests and hobbies too. Having your freedom in a relationship means that your partner should support your life outside the relationship and might not feel the need to know or be involved in every part of your life. And that means giving your partner the same freedom and independence. In other words, your relationship is balanced.

2. **You can talk to each other about anything and everything:**

They say that secrecy is the enemy of intimacy. And every healthy relationship is built on a foundation of honesty and trust. If you trust one another, you can be vulnerable and weak in their company because you recognize that instead of judging you, they will hold you and support you through the dark times. You're able to pour your heart out to them, no matter how stupid some things might sound. You don't keep secrets from each other. And when you're apart, you're not worried about them pursuing other people. You know they won't cheat or lie to you. You're safe and comfortable with them, knowing the fact that they won't ever hurt you, both physically or emotionally. You know they have your best interests in mind and respect you enough to encourage you to make your own choices. In conclusion, you respect each other's privacy, and the element of trust between you two comes naturally, and neither of you goes out of your way to work hard to "earn" their faith.

3. **You support and encourage each other's passions and ambitions:**

If your partner expresses his interest to become Batman, then you should assure that you'll hold the cape for him. If it's essential for them to, it should be important to you too, no matter how strange or bizarre their goals may sound. Even if you don't see eye to eye on something or have plans that aren't the same, healthy relationships are built on mutual inspiration and motivation; your partner should encourage you to be your best self, to face complex challenges, and to change the world, all by being there with you, supporting you through it all.

4. **You accept them for who they are:**

One of the most critical factors contributing to a healthy relationship is that you don't try to fix the other person. Love is all about seeing the flaws and blemishes of your partner and accepting them. It is about abiding by the bad habits and mannerisms of your significant other and working around them. It is about recognizing all the fears and insecurities and reassuring and comforting them. We all go through our bad days. We should strive to hold them in their bad days and dance and celebrate with them in their good ones. None of us are perfect; we're made with cracks and smudges, our souls have been shattered, and our skin is patchwork. There's nothing wrong with that. When your partner is broken, Vow to hold him together, and when your time comes, to be broken, beaten, restless, except that he'll keep you too.

5. **Playfulness and Light-heartedness:**

Healthy relationships are full of laughter and fun. It all comes down to joking and roasting each other playfully and laughing your hearts out. The spontaneity and adventures that you both might bring would eventually spice up your relationship. Sometimes one of you, or both of you, might feel emotionally or physically drained, or the challenges or distress might affect your relationship's tone. But being able to relieve the tension and share lighter moments, even briefly, strengthens your connection even in tough times.

6. **Conflict Resolution:**

Even in a healthy relationship, you'll have occasions where you might agree to disagree. It's entirely normal for couples to have disagreements and feel frustrated or angry with their partner. But that doesn't mean you should disrespect your partner based on his opinions and thinking. It all comes down to how you choose to address the conflict. You and your partner must talk about your differences politely, honestly, and with respect. Know when you or your partner is wrong, and apologize rightfully for it. You should be open to change too. Your number 9 might look like a number 6 to your partner, but it doesn't mean your partner is wrong. It simply means you both are looking at the same thing from different perspectives. Couples should try to understand each other, make their points apparent, and then sort out whatever's bothering them.

7. **You feel at ease talking about your past:**

Our past might be filled with our darkest secrets, but it does, in no way, defines us. When you feel free to tell your partner all about your exes, and the time you got depressed, and any failures or rejections that you received in your past, it shows that you trust your partner completely. Everything that has happened to your history has brought you to where you are today and changed you into a completely different person. Your partner should reassure you, and you shouldn't feel the need to hide any details from them. Similarly, you should comfort your partner and give them the same assurance.

8. **You share responsibilities:**

A relationship should always be based on equality. Putting the same effort into the success of the relationship is vital. Yes, sometimes your partner may do their 80%, and you have to put in your 120% and vice versa, but being on the same page and sharing all the responsibilities are a significant sign of a healthy relationship. One of you might be over-responsible in certain things, and one of you might be under-responsible in certain things, and it could be the other way around too. The over/under responsible dynamic is natural. However, when it becomes unbalanced, it can set off a cycle of anger, guilt, hurt, and resentment. Making sure of your particular dynamic and working on your responsibilities allows you to grow as an individual and a couple and balance things out.

9. **Making your partner feel loved:**

You value your partner's emotions and make them feel accepted and important. You ask them about their day, tell them about yours, and listen attentively to whatever they have to say. You both spend quality time together and make memories that you know you'll cherish forever. You never hesitate to try new things with them, maybe go to a restaurant you guys never go to before or go on a spontaneous trip to another city or country. It might be a shared hobby, too, like joining a dance class, jogging daily, or sitting over a cup of coffee. You surprise each other with dates and gifts. And even though the gift might not be that expensive, your partner will hold onto it forever.

10. **Your relationship has gotten stronger over time:**

The ultimate sign that your relationship is sustainable for the long term is that it only grew stronger with time. No matter how many times your partner has pissed you off or annoyed you, you couldn't help but fall in love with them a little more every day. Your relationship has slowly built, developing deeper roots with each passing year. The great David

King of Hearts

Foster Wallace once said, "The essential kind of freedom involves attention and awareness and discipline, and being able to care about other people truly and to sacrifice for them over and over in myriad petty, unsexy ways every day."

In conclusion, if you relate to the signs above, consider yourself lucky and cling to your partner for as long as your destiny would allow.

If you found this video helpful, don't forget to like, subscribe, comment, and share this with someone important to you. I hope you learned something valuable today. Take care, have a good rest, and till the next video ☺

1.

Chapter 3:
10 Signs Someone Has A Crush On You

Have that inkling suspicion that someone likes you but you're not 100% sure about it?

Many of you will agree that there is a certain level of thrill and adrenaline rush when it comes to crushing on someone. It could also lead to feelings of anxiety and nervousness as well.

I'm sure you've been in a similar situation before – where you had a crush on someone and not know how to express or be yourself around that person. But at the same time secretly hoping he or she knows you're attracted to them so that you may begin a romantic relationship with them.

What if you're on the receiving end of that crush, how do you identify the signs and signals that the person is sending you?

Here are 10 Signs that someone has a crush on you:

1. There is a distinct difference in their behavior when they are around you.

It may not be obvious or easily noticeable, but the guy or girl who is secret crushing on you will most likely be nervous when they are around you, or when they engage you in conversation. They might act shy or coy, and maybe even blush when looking at you.

On the flip side, they might also be more enthusiastic in their approach towards you - by expressing cheerfulness because one some level, you make them happy. A person who likes you will pay more attention to the minor details of what you say and what you do. They might also try to make sure you feel great because they want you to feel comfortable and at ease around them as well.

2. They might notice you from a distance.

A person who has a crush on you will likely try to peek a gaze at you from a distance. Whether you are at the same workplace, gym, or friendly hangouts with other friends, if you catch them looking at you more than usual, that is a very big sign that is pointing in your favor. They are also likely to spend a longer time gazing at you or giving you some serious eye contact.

In the digital age, distance could also be in the form of internet presence. They might also try to look you up on your social media channels. A good way to tell is if they start liking your posts and commenting on them. That is their way of entering into your life without being too obvious about it.

3. They will always find excuses to come close or talk.

You can easily understand whether someone is interested in you or not by their enthusiasm for interacting with you. Whether it is trying to match their timings for going to the coffee break with you or adjusting their dates with their friends to take you out to the movie, they will never leave one opportunity to chance to spend that golden time with you. They might also find the silliest of reason for just starting a conversation with you - like asking whether you will teach them something new or bring them somewhere for a meal.

4. Everything you do is appreciated by them.

As a crush, their goal is to make you notice them. To show you that they deserve your attention and time.

If you are going through a bad day, count on your potential crush to talk to you or to make an effort to help you feel better. It is highly likely that your crush will try their best to encourage and make you laugh as well.

They might also laugh at your silliest of jokes. Take it as a form of flattery as it shows that they want to win you over. At the end of the day, as long as it is genuine, it is always better to be around someone who helps you feel good at the end of the day.

5. Lets you know they are always available when you need them.

Another sign that your crush likes you is that they will make themselves available to you as and when you might want to talk. They might be quick to reply your messages when you text them, and they will find time for you whenever they can to engage you in conversations that lets them get to know you more. They might also throw in some hints there to show their interest in you.

6. Makes excuses to touch you!

If someone has a crush on you, they will definitely express interest by engaging in physical contact with you. Be it just as an excuse to feel the soft sweat shirt you are wearing or turning your wrist to appreciate your watch, watch out for these signs. Physical touch is a sign of flirting, and you need to pay attention to them. If they go one step further by poking you or touching you from the back, it is a sure-fire way to know that your someone likes you.

7. Surprise you!

This might not happen with everyone, but there are some people who likes the art of gifting! Especially when they like someone they want to make them feel special, be it bringing them their favorite chocolates and flowers, treating you to a meal, buying you your favorite drink, or getting you something you told them you liked during the last conversation. These are signs that they are paying attention to the little details about you, and that they are trying to express their attraction for you in the form of gift-giving. Friends don't usually buy things for you for no reason at all, so pay attention to this!

8. Borrowing things.

This sign may be rare as well but it could happen. It may sound cliché but when we like someone, we want to keep their things close to us. Any items which belong to you will be special to the person who likes you! Borrowing things could be their way of engaging in interaction with you as well, especially if they are very shy to ask you out.

9. They Compliment your appearance and dressing.

An easy way to know if someone has a crush on you is if they have nice compliments for the clothes you are wearing, for the styling of your hair, or just simply saying you look good today. We say the same when we go on dates to someone we find attractive. We give them compliments to show the other party that we are interested in them. The next time you receive a compliment from someone you suspect has a crush on you, take note of this point.

10. They Ask You Out

If your crush likes you, he or she will most likely ask when you are free to go for a meal or to watch a movie together. They might want to take this time to get you to notice them as more than friends. If they engage in any of the previous 9 signs we have discussed, you could potentially be on a date without even knowing it. So watch out for the signs carefully!.

If however, you are emotionally unavailable, it is perfectly okay to let your crush know at any point that you are not ready for a relationship if you see it being a potential cause of issue for your friendship with them. Ensure that you first confirm that they do indeed have a crush on you before you take any drastic actions to reject them if you are uninterested.

Now that you know what those signs are, you will know how to respond if someone has a crush on you. Do what you will with the information, just do go breaking too many hearts!

Chapter 4: 10 Ways To Build A Strong Relationship

Relationships are not always easy, especially when both people aren't exactly on the same page. But the key to a strong and healthy relationship doesn't necessarily mean you guys are mirror images of each other when it comes to your opinions and personality. Understanding and adaptability is the key to a successful relationship.

When it comes down to the two people involved, no two relationships are the same. As we are unique individuals, so will our relationships be as well. The needs, goals, perceptions, and growth vary from couple to couple. With that in mind, we are going to talk about the 10 signs that point to a strong relationship that all couples should strive for at some point in their time together.

1. Trust.

The foundation of any relationship is very much dependent on trust. More than love, trust is more important for the bond to be strong. Trust includes honesty, integrity, and at the same time feeling safe and comfortable with the person that you are with.

Trust has to be earned over time, by proving to your partner that they can count on you to be faithful in the relationship and also to be honest with things that are going on with your life.

Trust is also earned when you work with your partner in the same domain and you have a clear understanding of their passions.

2. Respect for personal space.

I feel that this needs to be heard loud and clear. Being in a relationship does not imply breathing down the neck of your partner all the time.

Doing so could potentially suffocate the other person and make the relationship bitter over time.

I am sure you don't like your personal space to be violated by someone else all the time, so expect the same adverse reactions if you do that to your partner as well.

It is very important that each individual in the relationship has the utmost respect for the other person's private space. Allowing room to breathe can be a wonderful way to recharge and come back to the relationship with renewed excitement and interest.

3. Spending quality time with your partner.

It is very important for two people in a relationship to spend quality time together. A certain time each week that you have set aside for your partner where the two of you will focus only on each other and nothing else. A time when you ask your partner the deep questions, to engage in insightful thought, or to simply be mindfully present in each other's company. It is an amazing feeling when your significant other engages you by asking about your day, asking how you are feeling, and making sure you are well taken care of.

While many thinks that quantity of time is important as well, I would argue that this could lead to complacency. It is important that you don't treat spending time with your partner by counting the hours, but by counting the moments instead.

4. Encouraging each other to achieve personal goals.

When your partner becomes your life coach who motivates you to become a better person every day and achieve your personal goals , this is where the bond grows beyond the surface level feelings into a much deeper emotional and spiritual connection.

By understanding the kind of service you need to provide to your partner to support their goals and dreams, you are in effect helping them achieve what they truly want in life. This proactiveness will make them fall in love with themselves and with you even more.

5. Physical Intimacy.

Physical intimacy doesn't necessarily imply sex. Sex is not necessary for a relationship to stick on provided both sides are on the same page. Even cuddles, hugs, and kissing your partner is an act of intimacy that is very important in any relationship. It is very crucial to have that understanding in the bedroom and to be able to openly express your needs, your desires, and your fantasies, and your inhibitions regarding physical intimacy with your partner. Lack of physical touch could result in loss of intimacy away from the bedroom. So be mindful that you keep that in check in your relationship.

6. Communication.

There is nothing more important than keeping the communication flowing with your partner. If you aren't comfortable in sharing your deepest emotions, fears, and insecurities with that person, you should probably think about why that is so. Your better half should not just be your partner in a relationship but should ideally by a very close and personal friend as well. There should not be inhibitions about expressing one's feelings and opinions about a matter out of fear that it might end up in a fight with the other person. Fights will inevitably happen in every relationship. How you manage the fights is what makes or breaks your strong bond.

7. Teamwork.

A relationship would become a burden if one person is constantly working hard to keep the other person comfortable and the other one doesn't contribute much. As the saying goes, team work makes the dream work. Be it household chores, cleaning the dishes, settling the bills, taking the dog out for a dump, both have to contribute equally for it to be a balanced relationship. Both will need to take the initiative to help out the other party where possible otherwise resentment and unhappiness might follow.

8. Personal Time.

This point overlaps quite a bit with providing personal space.

To be a more balanced individual, you really need to have that "me-time" for yourself. Time where you spend alone. Time where you engage in your favourite hobbies or sports that you might not share with your partner.

Giving yourself that "me-time" can also include having that favorite cup of coffee while watching your favorite shows, catching up with your friends, cooking your favorite meal, or watching your favorite team match. Once you start balancing time for yourself you start respecting your partner's personal space and time as well, and that gives the relationship a breath of fresh air and keeps you both going.

9. Talking to your partner, not to other people.

It is very easy in times of fights to simply run away from the problems you are facing and into your friends for shelter. While having a strong social support network is great to have, always ensure that you come back to the relationship with a clear mind and talk things through openly and without fear of judgement.

Miscommunications are usually high up on the list when it comes to disagreements. It is always best to sort out the differences there instead of running away and letting the situation escalate to an unresolvable point.

10. The 3 golden phrases.

Yes, you are right. In a relationship, you should be able to say 'I am sorry', 'Thank you', and 'I love you' as much as possible. Being able to express your love, regret, appreciativeness, and sorrow, will enlighten the bond between you and your partner. By verbally saying these words regularly, you are showing your partner that you can be vulnerable around them and that they can be the same with you.

A Strong relationship is not easy to build, but it is worth the effort if we take the time and effort to put into practice some of these points that we have discussed today. Take care and I'll see you in the next one.

Chapter 5:
10 Signs You're Not Ready To Be In A Relationship

Do you feel the societal pressure to date but can't get yourself into it? Or if you have started dating, ever wondered why your dates go well but you never hear from the person again? Or why despite your best efforts, you can't keep a relationship working? But maybe the problem isn't out there but within yourself.

A relationship can either be the most beautiful thing in your life or the worst. It's not always candlelight dinners and a bed of roses. It requires a strong sense of responsibility and commitment to your significant other. You may feel like you're doing your best, but there are a few factors you should consider that might be keeping your relationships at a distance.

1. **You get overly dependent on people.**

Being emotionally dependent on people sometimes is normal as it is in humans' nature to get reassurance every once in a while. But getting utterly relied on a person to make yourself feel better about yourself can get you nowhere. Your emotions shouldn't be driven by what others might feel or think about you, instead solely by how they will affect you. No one can define your self-worth better than yourself. Try to avoid being too clingy and needy and keep a safe distance from the people you love so you might not annoy them.

2. **Your insecurities reflect on your behavior.**

Whether you have insane trust issues or you feel like you're not good enough, you start showing the signs of your insecurities in your behavior. You start overthinking everything that your partner does; even a slight change in his/her tone is enough to keep yourself wide awake at night. You get incredibly jealous even if your partner does so much as breathe in the direction of someone else. But as they say, that trust is the critical element of a relationship, so why not trust your significant other wholeheartedly and work on yourself to change your pattern of behaviors that may negatively affect your relationship.

3. **You can't stop analyzing your past relationship.**

This is perhaps the most crucial factor as to why relationships usually don't survive. You're still hung up on your ex and compare everything your new partner does to what your old partner used to do. You spend most of your time clinging to your past, daydreaming, or perhaps imagining the situations where you could've right all the wrongs. It's usually not fair to your new partner. Yes, it's not easy to just forget someone and move on, but don't get into a new relationship until and unless you're revived from the old one. Give yourself as much time as you want to murder those old feelings, and when you're done, get yourself out there and enjoy life.

4. **You try to change who they are as a person.**

Another reason that you can't get yourself into dating is that you're always looking for someone perfect, or if you've already found someone, you're molding them into someone they're not. You're always looking for someone with specific traits that you've written on your bucket list for a long time. You have created an ideal image about your significant other that your start losing your mind if something even minor deviates from it. But isn't love all about accepting someone with all their flaws and weaknesses? Instead, we should try to better ourselves first.

5. **You're afraid of a serious commitment.**

Maybe the idea of sharing your life and thoughts with someone scares you. You might think, Isn't it too soon to let someone see all of your goods and bad? You haven't fully experienced your life on your own yet. You want to travel the world or do academically better, or maybe you want to spend some alone time. Giving someone your time and energy and being there for them isn't your cup of tea at the moment.

The best you can do is be honest and tell them you're not ready for something serious yet.

6. **You don't love yourself enough and have serious self-doubts about yourself.**

We all go through our cynical phases where we feel like we're not worthy of love. But being in that constant phase might affect you terribly. You can't expect someone to love you if you don't even love yourself. Having self-doubts sometimes is normal too, but getting them to a point where your partner might feel irritated and it starts influencing your relationship isn't healthy. We should accept ourselves for who we are, take constructive criticism, and try to be a better person for what it's worth.

7. **You have your walls built up and are emotionally unavailable.**

You don't consider sharing your feelings and thoughts with people. You try to solve every problem independently and isolate yourself from your loved ones now and then. The moment a minor inconvenience happens, or you're upset about anything, you tend to distance yourself from everyone. You don't care enough about other's problems too but rather run from them. No one wants a partner who distances himself; instead, being vulnerable and weak looks attractive. It gives your significant other the confidence that you're true to them with your emotions.

8. You have poor communication skills.

Communication is as vital as any other thing when it comes to relationships. If you tend to keep something that bothers you and not express it, you might find yourself in a never-ending pit of overthinking and imagining the worst-case scenarios. Your partner may feel irritated by your constant behavior changes and not knowing the reasons behind them. Talking and sorting out the things concerning you anchors your relationship well and gives you a boost of confidence.

9. You think that a relationship is your prescription for boredom and loneliness.

Another primary reason why relationships don't last long these days is that people want to kill their boredom by acquainting with another person. They're bound to put in extra efforts just for the sake of their relationship working out and them not ending up alone. You're willing to make sacrifices just to make the other person happy. This affects your mental state as you're emotionally drained out and always looking for people to cope with your loneliness. But if you aren't happy single, you won't be as comfortable in a relationship too.

10. You're incredibly inconsistent with people.

One day you're making them feel like they're on top of the world, and the next day you're crashing them to the ground. You're confused about your feelings for them and are not treating them properly. You might act like the perfect person they can get your hands on, but another moment you might work like you don't even give two cents about them. This might leave your partner in a state of anxiousness and confusion because you're not fully committing to your feelings for them.

In conclusion, it's completely okay not to be in a relationship and not fall victim to societal norms if you're not ready. We should practice self-love before anything else, try to be at peace with ourselves first so that we might be able to bring peace into our partner's life too. I hope these points bring you a new self-awareness and you focus more on the attitude adjustments that will eventually guide you to a path to be ready.

If you found this video helpful, don't forget to like, subscribe, comment, and share this with someone important to you. I hope you learned something valuable today. Take care, have a good rest, and till the next video ☺

Chapter 6:
10 Signs You're Dating A Sociopath

Before discussing the signs that you're dating a Sociopath or not let's first understand the term sociopath. It'll make things even more digestible for you.

Currently, around 1 % of the US population is suffering from the personality disorders of Sociopathy. A sociopath disregards people, society, and important societal rules around them. They are extremely self-assured and think about being more talented and better looking than others. Think about Hannibal Lecter, Joker, Patrick Bateman, John Doe, the Buffalo Bill, and many others on the list. Are you a true devotee of Hollywood? Then visualize Charles Manson, Ted Bundy, and Jeffrey Dahmer in your mind. Yes, these are the most precise and realistic character roles of Sociopaths.

According to Dr. Scott A. Bond, Sociopathy is a learned behavior that is often the result of some form of childhood trauma.

Main

In today's video, we will be taking a closer look at the central signs to spot a sociopath so that you can make an informed decision on whether to leave the relationship or to stick it out despite knowing the risks.

1. They get Jealous

Mostly sociopaths get jealous of their partner and blame them for everything. You might find yourself defending against the continuous false accusations of your partner. They would never encourage you to pursue your dreams or achieve anything because of their never-ending jealousy.

2. They Lie about Everything

Lying is never okay under any circumstances; however, Sociopaths lie with every breath. They do it on a regular basis and without any regrets. They find themselves smart doing this because they figure that you might not even know. While trust should be the foundation of any relationship, Sociopaths seemingly lie to their partner with perfection and they are good at planning and telling a foolproof lie which can be difficult to even guess.

3. They are always Arrogant

They constantly consider that they are better than other people are. They are constant swaggers and like boasting about their running speed, nice clothes, or shoes. This attitude in the relationship could be extremely negative, abusive, and uncomfortable. You need to watch out if your partner is always invalidating you and bragging about their capabilities.

There is a possibility that they feel superior in every way and there is no one else that can match the same skill-set they own. If you tell them about their mistakes they will be annoyed and their arrogance in such situations will touch the skies. They might even feel portray that you have hurt their self-respect.

4. They don't think about Consequences

It is often exciting for people to engage in impulsive behavior sometimes, but sociopaths tend to participate in impulsive activities regularly. Apart from being dangerous, it can result in dealing with adverse financial consequences. The same goes in the decision-making process of a relationship. If your partner does not think about the negative consequences of their decision, then you might be dating a sociopath.

5. They don't want to Change

While most people learn from the mistakes and consequences of their poor actions, sociopaths don't pay attention to any of this. These people show zero desire to learn from their mistakes and bring positive change in their attitudes. Their consistently disregarding attitude will make it extremely challenging. Watch out for this sign.

6. They do not tag along with Rules

You may think that it can be exciting to break some rules in the beginning with your date, but if it is a regular occurrence, there may be something wrong there especially if it is an act that concerns criminal behavior. Be mindful that this can ruin your present and future. Watch out if your partner engages in reckless behaviors that are out of the norm and don't hesitate to bring it up with your closest friends and family if you find something amiss.

7. They do not Care

Yes, it is normal to have some days off, but you need to watch out if your partner never cares about anything. A healthy relationship is based upon mutual give and take. If your partner never empathizes with you, then the possibility is that you are in a relationship with someone who might only care about themselves. Since mutual care and kindness are the essences of a healthy relationship, these warning signs should ring some alarm bells for you that you may want to consider walking away from this relationship.

8. They are the Loners

Their antisocial personality makes it extremely difficult to make or maintain a close relationship with others. A sociopath shows extremely antisocial behavior with others and does not seem to have any desire to make any friends.

9. They Relentlessly Ruin Things

A sociopath prioritizes his or her needs over their partner and continuously looks for excitement above all else. They ruin everything with no one left to clean up the mess. If you are regularly facing financial crises left behind by your partner, then you might be dating a sociopath.

10. They have Impulsive Mood Swings

A characteristic trait of a sociopath is that they tend to have unstable or unexpected mood swings, expressing abrupt temperamental changes when things are not going their way. If you said something unexpected and your partner responds with controlling and manipulative behaviors, be careful as this could be another tell-tale sign.

Closing

If any of the above points rang any alarm bells in you, it is time to start paying close attention to these details. Start asking yourself the right questions. While you may have the inclination to give your partner the benefit of the doubt, never become too complacent and assume that you need to stay with someone who doesn't treat you like you rightfully deserve. If you believe that your partner is a sociopath, seek help, talk to a counsellor, your family member, or your close friends. They might be able to paint a clearer picture for you to make an informed decision on the next best move for you.

So, that's it for today's video. Did we miss out on any elements of a sociopath? Let us know in the comments section below. Do not forget to subscribe to our channel, like, and share this video.

Thank you!

Chapter 7:
10 Signs Your Crush Likes You

The weak knees you get when you see them, the fantastic smell of their cologne that you can't get enough of, the skipping of your heartbeat when you see their smile or hear their laughter, your face lighting up when you see their pictures. Yeah yeah, we know that feeling very well; YOU'VE GOT A CRUSH! It happens to almost all of us. Maybe there's a co-worker who caught your eye or a classmate that you exchange glances. Or perhaps it could be a total stranger that you have just met and pretty soon started liking them.

You keep thinking about them and their dreamy eyes, their pleasant bright smile, their oh so perfectly structured face, and their lips that are so... but wait! Aren't we getting too much ahead of ourselves?

Maybe, just maybe, they've shown some signs too. They say a crush is called so because they leave you feeling crushed if they don't reciprocate your feelings. But if you've wished upon your lucky star and maybe this time, your star took pity on you and have answered your prayer, then your case might become different than the one I just mentioned. Getting suffocating and thought-provoking mixed signals from your crush might drive you crazy. You are always left wondering, hoping if the indicative signs mean anything. That may be your crush likes you back too. If you are plucking the poor petals of your hundredth rose and enchanting, 'He loves me/He loves me not,' then save it for later, pretty please?

We are here for you, and using our expertise, we will help you figure out if you are your crush's crush too.

Here are ten signs (in no particular order) that will help you analyze if your crush likes you back:

1. **Their eyes are fixated on you:**

They say that the eyes are windows to the soul. A study has found out that people unconsciously fixate their eyes on the things they want the most. People tend to keep eye contact with someone they like, apart from the few shy ones who might not like its intensity; perhaps when you will catch them looking at you, they will look away and blush. But shy or not, you have to notice their pupils. Studies show that an individual's pupil dilates when they see someone they like. They also tend to blink more often while watching their crush. If you feel like you are being stared at by your crush or catches them stealing glances at you, and they smile afterward, then consider yourself lucky. And if he's directly locking eyes while talking to you, then that's just the cherry on top of your sundae!

2. **Notice their body language:**

It is said that actions speak louder than words. Have you ever noticed how you feel around them? Do you get nervous, hyper, shy, or suddenly quiet? Or most importantly, if your crush feels the exact same emotions around you. If he gets flustered or fidgets a little more than usual, or starts to blush or sweat while talking to you, then maybe it's a sign he likes you back. You should also notice that when your crush is standing with you, his feet must be pointing towards you. Weird right?

But hey, I don't make the rules. When we are interested in someone, our body naturally leans towards them to be closer. This is a subconscious action that signifies interest. So, the next time you're having a conversation with your crush, notice if he leans in and sits forward with his arms uncrossed, having constant eye contact and listening to you attentively.

3. **They're not afraid to open up to you:**

It's normal to develop trust issues considering we suffer from terrible experiences, like heartbreaks and betrayals, in our lives. We might have built a protective wall around ourselves to keep people from hurting us. But when we are around someone we trust, those walls come crumbling down without us even realizing it. Whether it's about them spending their next vacations abroad, or their future college plans, or maybe their deepest darkest secrets, they don't hesitate to talk about all of it to you. Experts say, vulnerability nurtures attraction and develops a sense of trust by fostering deeper feelings of closeness. So, if your crush is vulnerable and weak around you and does not shy pouring out their heart to you, then you must be someone really special to them.

4. **They want to know a lot more about you:**

From your favorite color to your favorite food, to your favorite book, and even your grandma's birthday! They want to know every single detail about you. They remember the important dates and details of your life, even those that subconsciously slipped out from your tongue. Not only this, they never get tired from hearing about you and asking all about you. They might even watch your favorite tv show or read your favorite book to impress you. They make small gestures from the particulars that you have told them. And they are always looking for more opportunities to get to know you better.

5. **Always willing to help you:**

Men thrive on solving women's problems. I guess it's something biological that men always feel the need to provide for the women he cares about, and vice versa. Whether it's giving her his jacket in the cold or her bringing him warm soup when he's feeling down, it all comes down to how much the individual cares about the other person. Your crush eagerly offers you help with just anything and is always available to lend you a hand whenever you need it. The term 'hero instinct' has been given to men who are always ready to help the women of their liking.

6. **They preen themselves around you:**

As soon as you enter the room, you see them adjust their clothes, sleek back their hair, or touch their face, then know that they are trying to look presentable and impressive in front of you. Preening around the people we like is a subconscious way to advertise our romantic interest. We tend to want to look the best around them. From wearing our best outfits to smelling fresh and pleasant and making efforts to make oneself look attractive.

7. **They become flirty/playful around you:**

Another thing to notice is that if your crush is being flirtatious or funny around you. They might try to get your attention and show affection by being playful in a light-hearted and silly way. They might even call you funny nicknames, tease you, or joke around you. It might also be a sarcastic comment or a light punch on the arm or simply laughing with you on random stuff.

8. Their friends act weird when you're around:

If your crush's friends start acting weird when they see you, the chances are that your crush has already told them about you (which, by the way, is basically guaranteed. I mean, who does not say to their friends about their love interest?). Anyways, look for the signs as to how their friends act when you are near them. Do they say their name out loud? Do they giggle or whisper to each other? Do they give you two a playful smile and leave you two alone? Do they randomly start to tell you great things about your crush? Or maybe, they might even ask point-blank if you like the person!
As for you, play along, and maybe their friends would get some sense into them, and they will finally as you out.

9. They try to be always near you:

Do you ever go to a party, hang out with your group of friends, or go to any gathering for that matter but always end up beside your crush? Or perhaps they're making excuses and efforts to see you more often, like a mistaking call or text that results in them asking you out. This might be another sign that your crush likes you; that is, they are trying to get into your proximity. They will try and make sure to spend as much time as they can with you. Whether it's about trying that new restaurant or studying for the English test together, you will see them hovering around you quite often.

10. Their mood changes when you hang out with someone else:

Suppose you are engaged in a deep, meaningful conversation, walking side by side, or just simply laughing with someone from the opposite sex, and you catch your crush feeling gloomy and staring intensely at you both, or walking out of the room, or even joining you guys. In that case, chances are they might be feeling protective or jealous. They want to get all your attention and not share you with anyone else, which is highly adorable. But beware! There is a difference between being playfully jealous and being full-on psychotic possessiveness, which is a huge red flag, and you should probably then stay away from them.

In the end, it is advisable not to assume anything based on just signs and to gut up and tell them how you feel about them. If they reciprocate your feelings, then good for you. If not, then trust me, it'll not be the end of the world; at least you'll be sure of their feelings towards you. And remember, there's always someone out there who would want to be with you. You'll just have to wait and see where destiny will take you.

If you found this video helpful, don't forget to like, subscribe, comment, and share this with someone important to you. I hope you learned something valuable today. Take care, have a good rest, and till the next video ☺

PART 2

Chapter 1:
10 Signs You're Falling In Love

As our Literature master, Shakespeare, once said, 'A heart to love, and in that heart, courage, to make's love known.'

Ah, love! A four-lettered small word that leaves such a heavy impact on people. Falling in love is nothing short of a beautiful experience, but it can also give you a veritable roller-coaster of emotions. From feeling unsure to terrifying, disgusting, exhilarating, and excited, you might feel it all. If your mobile screen pops up and you're hoping to see their name on the screen, or you're looking for their face in a crowd full of thousands, then you, my child, are doomed! You are well familiar with the feeling of getting butterflies just by hearing their voice, the urge to change your wardrobe completely to impress them, the constant need to be with them all the time. It is known that people who are in love tend to care about the other person's needs as they do their own.

You often go out of their way for their happiness. Whether it's something as small as making their favorite dish or impressing them with some grand gestures, you always try to make them feel content and happy.

If you're in the middle of some casual inquiry into whether you're falling in love, then we are here to help you. Below are some signs for you to discover if it's really just simply a loss of appetite or if you're merely lovesick.

1. **You don't hesitate to try new things with them:**

One of the factors that you could look into is that you become fearless and more adventurous when you are in love. You don't hang back to step out of your comfort zone and engage in all your partner favors' activities and interests. Suddenly the idea of trying sushi or wearing something bright doesn't seem so crazy. You are willing to be more daring and open to new experiences. You are ready to go on that spontaneous trip with them and make memories, all while being a little scared inside. But isn't love all about trying new things with your partner? The New York Times article in 2008 revealed that people in a relationship who try new hobbies together help keep the spark alive long after the honeymoon phase is over.

2. **You're always thinking about them:**

When you are in love, you always tend to think about your partner. Rehash your last conversation with them, or simply smiling at something they said, or questions like what they must be doing right now, have they eaten their meal yet, did they go to work on time or were late again, are always on the back of your mind. You are mentally, emotionally, and physically impacted about caring for them. But it isn't overwhelming. Instead, you get a sense of a calm and secure reality that you will constantly crave. When in love, we tend to merge with that person in such a way that they start to dominate our thoughts and we become wholly preoccupied with them.

3. You become anxious and stressed:

According to a psychology study, falling in love could also cause higher levels of cortisol, a stress home, in your body. So the next time you feel jittery or anxious, that person might mean more to you than you think. You might become anxious to dress up nicely to impress them, or if they ask you something, the pressure of answering them intellectually can be expected. But suppose you're feeling overly anxious about your partner, like them not texting you back instantly or thinking they might be cheating on you. In that case, it's an indication of insecure attachment, and you might want to work on yourself to avoid feeling like this.

4. You become inspired and motivated:

A few days ago, you needed the motivation to get out of bed. And now, the future suddenly seems so bright and full of potential. Your partner inspires you to set up new goals, have a positive attitude, and cheer you from behind while you feel full of energy and chase them. When we are in love, a part of our brain, considered the reward system, releases excess dopamine, and we feel invincible, omnipotent, and daring. Your life becomes significantly better when you're around them.

5. You become empathetic towards them:

It's not a secret that you start seeing your partner as an extension of yourself and reciprocate whatever they feel when you fall in love. Suppose they are accepted into their favorite program, or they expect to receive that interview call, or their favorite football team might have lost in the quarters. In that case, you might feel the same excitement, happiness, or distress that your partner does. Becoming empathetic towards your partner means making sacrifices for them, like going to the grocery store because your partner is tired or refueling their tank in the cold so that they don't have to step out. According to an expert, "Your love is growing when you have an increased sense of empathy toward your partner. When they feel sad, you feel sad. When they feel happy, you feel happy. This might mean going out of the way to give them love in the way that they want to receive it, even if it is not the way you would want to receive love."

6. **It's just plain easy:**

You don't have to put in extra effort, and it doesn't seem to drain your energy. Instead, you feel energized and easy. You can be your complete, authentic self around them. And it always just seems to go with the flow. Even the arguments don't feel much heated as they did in the other relationships. When you're in love, you prioritize your partner over your pride and ego. You don't hesitate to apologize to them and keep your relationship above everything. When you are with your partner, and it doesn't feel like hard work, know that they are the one!

7. **You crave their presence:**

Some theorists say that we are more drawn to kissing, hugging, and physical touch when we fall in love. Physical closeness releases a burst of the love hormone termed Oxytocin, which helps us feel bonded. Of course, you don't want to come as someone too clingy who is permanently attached to his partner's hip, but knowing where your person is or how their day went is what you should be looking forward to. On the flipside, Corticotrophin is released as part of a stress response when we are away from our partner, which can contribute to anxiety and depression.

8. You feel safe around them:

It takes a lot of courage for people to open up to their partners. If you don't mind being vulnerable around them, or if you've opened up to them about your dark past or addressed your insecurities, and they have listened contently to you and reassured you. You have done vice versa with your partner, then that's just one of the many signs that you both are in love with each other. Long-lasting love gives you a solid ground and a safe space where you can be upset and vulnerable. When we feel an attachment to our partner, our brain releases the hormones vasopressin and Oxytocin, making us feel secure.

9. You want to introduce them to your family and friends:

You just never shut up about your love interest over the family dinner or when hanging out with your friends. They know all about them, from their favorite spot in the city to the color of their eyes, to how much you adore them and want to spend every single minute talking about them. And now all your family members and friends are curious to meet the guy/girl they have been listening about for the past few weeks. You want to introduce them into every aspect of your life and want it to last this time. So, you make perfect arrangements for them to meet your friends and family, and on the other hand, threatens them to behave Infront of him/her.

10. You care about their happiness:

When you put them and their feelings first, that's how you know it's true love. You don't just want happiness for yourself only, but instead wants it in excess measure for your partner. According to marriage researchers at UC Berkeley, " Spouses who love each other stay together longer, be happier, and support each other more effectively than couples who do not love each other compassionately." You want to go out of your way, or do their favorite thing, to see a smile on their face.

Conclusion:

If you relate to the signs above, then you've already been hit by the love cupid. Scientists have discovered that falling in love, is in fact, a real thing. The brain releases Phenylethylamine, a hormone known for creating feelings of infatuation towards your significant other. The mix and match of different hormones released in our body while we are in love are wondrous. If you have gotten lucky and found a special someone for yourself, then cling to them and don't let them go! If you found this video helpful, please like and subscribe to the channel. Also don't forget to share this video with someone who you find might benefit from this topic as well!

Chapter 2: What To Do When Your Partner Cheats On You

We all know someone who has been cheated on or someone who did the cheating, or maybe there is a chance that someone cheated on you. When something like this happens, everyone involved in this gets disturbed. When you find out that your significant other cheated on you, you feel betrayed, and the first emotion you show is anger, and you just want to leave; fight or flight is a natural response. A therapist says that you should never make an instant decision because once you calm down, you will see that there is a lot to lose, and you might also have children to consider. However, you will be conflicted as to what you should do. Here are some of the things you should do once you find out your partner is cheating.

1. Assess Your Partner's Attitude Regarding Cheating

Some people cheat as a one-time thing, and some have entire relationships on their hiding side. Whether it is an isolated thing or something that happens regularly, you should have a heart-to-heart with your partner whenever you find about it. When you are doing that, you should pay attention to their attitude, notice if your partner is in denial, make excuses, or blame you. If they do that, this means they are not ready to change. Still, if your partner is ashamed and recognizes they have a problem and are ready to change that, that is a good sign.

2. Speak to a Couple's Therapist

However, as much as you may speak to your therapist about your cheating partner, going to one with your partner can likewise help decide whether both of you can find ways to work things out. Also, you may think about how you'll at any point have the option to trust your better half once more, and an objective party could help you sort it out. "Conceding and remedying awful conduct, revamping trust, and pardoning are the principal issues you need to confront," Most of the time, affairs occur because the communication and intimacy in the relationship have broken down. Both parties must approach the problem with a sincere wish to discover what went wrong and fix it. Forgiveness is an important part of the healing process, whether the couple stays together or not. A therapist said, "While I don't think you should stay together and suffer if nothing's working, in my practice, I see many couples who do the work and wind up happier than before."

3. Ask Yourself If You Can Forgive Them

It is not easy to forgive someone who has cheated on you, but if you want to continue your relationship with them, that is the necessary part. Forgiving, of course, does not mean that you condone what happened or that it would be fine if it happens again but actually, what it means is that you want to close this chapter and move on. It is essential to create mutual forgiveness. Else, you will be stuck in blaming each other and defending yourself, and you will never be able to move forward from there.

4. Figure Out If You Still Love Each Other

Sometimes, love trumps everything, but other times, it's not enough. "Do you still love each other, and is it mutual? "Love is a lot more like a partnership than romance. Loving each other means focusing on what you want from your partner and being concerned with their happiness, too. Discussing <u>how you give and receive love</u> will improve your relationship and help you understand what makes each of you feel loved and express love effectively. The foundation of lasting love is the ability to work through things together."

Chapter 3:
How To Survive A Long Distance Relationship

Today we're going to talk about a very touchy yet important subject. If you have a partner who's not local, or you know that they are going to move countries some day, you've gotta be prepared for that time to come. You've got to be sure whether you will begin a long distance relationship or whether you will move to that country to be with that person.

For the purpose of this video, I am going to assume that you have already committed to being in a long distance relationship. And as with any commitment, you have got to be willing to make compromises and sacrifices to maintain that relationship.

There are a couple of things that you will have to mentally prepare yourself for if you are in it for the long haul with this person. They could be gone for days, weeks, months, or even years. First of all you have to ask yourself, are you okay with seeing this person only once every few months? Will you be happy if you wont be able to spend majority of the time with the person throughout the year? How will you cope with the distance? Are you okay with not having physical intimacy with the person? Will you be willing to sacrifice your freedom to wait for this person to return? And can you trust this person to be faithful to you as you spend all your time apart?

For me personally, I was committed to a Long distance relationship once before. And it was the hardest thing for me to do. Especially when it came time at the airport for the send off.

Having already known prior that it would happen someday, i still went ahead with the relationship. All was well and all was fun, but time soon caught up with us and before i knew it, it was already time to say goodbye... temporarily at least. I must admit that it was tough... It was tough because we have gotten so used to spending time together physically in the same space for so long, that this sudden transition was all foreign territory to me. Not being able to touch each other, not being able to meet up for meals, not being able to just hang out at the movies, and not to mention the time zone difference. These were all very real challenges. And they were incredible hard especially in the first few months. I cried at the airport, i cried on the drive home, I was incredibly unhappy, and i was not prepared in any capacity whatsoever to feel this way. You never really know how to feel about something until it actually happens to you.

Knowing that the next time we would see each other would be months away, there was no way to know how to feel or act when suddenly it feels like a limb has been chopped off and you are just struggling to find your feet again. I looked to friends for social support and that was the thing that got me through the toughest periods. Sure we could still

FaceTime and call and whatever. Especially in this day and age, but it was still tough having a relationship over the computer. It does feel like on some level you're dating virtually. Everything had to change and I had to relearn what it meant to be in a relationship all over again. I wasn't ever a sappy or clingy boyfriend. I know that about myself. But I do have an expectation to meet up maybe once or twice in a week. Now it's once or twice a year. And it's not fun at all.

So now I put that question back to you, after hearing this part of the story, are you willing to put yourself through this? Or would it be easier if you just chose someone who is in the same physical space with you with no plans on leaving town. If you were to ask me, I might actually do it all over again with someone like that.

The next thing that you've got to have to survive a long distance relationship, is to have a strong social support group. A group of friends that you can share your troubles with. People who can empathise with you, and people who can spend time with you in lieu of your partner. You never want to be in a situation where your partner is your entire world, because when they leave, you will most likely crumble. If you relied on them for all your happiness, their sudden absence will certainly leave you devastated. If u do not have a strong support network of friends, i would suggest you think doubly hard about committing to a long distance relationship.

Now comes the most important part, in my opinion, of having a successful long distance relationship. And that is trust. Trust in each other to be faithful, and trust in each other to do the right thing at all times.

I will bring back to my experience with my long distance relationship. To keep things short, after about a year into my LDR, i discovered that my partner had been cheating on me many times over. And my whole world did come crashing down. Having thought that everything was going according to plan up until that point, i was completely blindsided by the avalanche that hit me. It really hit me hard. But I knew that i loved myself more, and so I packed my bags and flew back home from the trip.

Getting over the relationship was relatively easy because i knew there was nothing left there anymore. There was no more trust to come home to. I had no faith in the relationship anymore and it was effectively over for me. It may sound too easy watching this video, but trust me i went through a great deal and I was incredibly happy with my decision. I learned that i was incredibly resilient and that even though things didn't work out the way i had hoped, and even though my vision of the future was changed drastically, it didn't knock me down. And I chose myself first.

So my question that I put to you now is, to what extent do you trust your partner to be faithful to you? Has he or she cheated on you before? Have they always chosen you first? Can you touch your heart and say they will never do anything to hurt you? Or are you too naive like I was to believe that all is well? Because I was incredibly confident at one point that we were making the LDR work beautifully. Until it suddenly didn't. Would you be okay if you found out that your partner was cheating on you secretly overseas while you guys were apart? Would you be paranoid of the things he could do? If you can answer these things honestly, then u might be able to LDR make it work for you. If not, again, do reconsider your relationship now.

For me personally, If you don't know my stance by now, I absolutely do not believe in LDR. Especially if it's a permanent period. If your partner is gone maybe for a 3-6 month work trip. Yeah maybe that's doable, but if they are gone for 5-6 years and if there's a big question mark behind that... I would totally back away. It would be a deal breaker for me.

The thing with relationships is that, I believe it is the physical presence, the physical connection, the physical communication, and the physical touch that keeps two people together. Without any of these things on a regular basis, it is likely that a couple with drift apart on some level... And without these things, one might be tempted to seek comfort and physical intimacy elsewhere if they can't wait another 5 months before they can see you again.

But if your foundation is incredibly strong, if you guys have made a commitment, if you guys trust each other completely, and if you believe that your relationship can weather any storm, then I already think that you know you can handle a long distance relationship. I am simply here to affirm to you what you already know.

But take me as a word of warning that even strong relationships do fail in the face of a long distance relationship. So you have to be prepared to handle anything that comes your way.

I hope I have been able to shed some light into this topic for you.

Take care and I'll see you in the next one.

Chapter 4:
What Happens When You Get Bored In A Relationship

Being bored in your relationship can make you feel unpleasant emotions; you would not feel like yourself. You will be more likely to be over things that excited you before, like sex, date night, vacation with your partner, etc. Even if you don't feel like ending things, the lack of satisfaction would be enough to get you frustrated and ready to break up. Due to this boredom, you may feel stuck in a tedious cycle or feel suffocated. There are many things you will notice about yourself when you are bored of your relationship.

Picking unnecessary fights with your partner is one of the signs that you are bored with them. Dr. Binita Amin, a clinical psychologist, says getting into arguments for innocuous reasons might signify you are bored. If you find yourself bickering with your partner for petty reasons, then you may want to step back and assess why. Boredom can efficiently fuel arguments, but disagreements happen in any relationship; the best way is to see if these arguments are indeed caused by boredom.

Your frustration with your relationship causes these arguments. You can always figure out what is exactly causing this boredom, and maybe you can overcome this problem and carry out a healthy relationship.

Sometimes, we all enjoy comfortable silence, but is that silence comfortable anymore, or is it just because you have no more to speak to each other. Silent meals even when you are in a sit-in restaurant, or even if a few words are exchanged, but those words are in safe and predictable confines, then that is a sign that you are bored. To prevent this, you can try strengthening your bond with your partner.

When we first meet a person we like or at the beginning of a relationship, we put our best self forward, we try to be perfect for them, but when a person feels bored, they no longer place any effort into their relationship. They don't bother looking nice for a date night or don't bother waiting for them at the dinner table because we all know such factors lead to a healthy relationship. Being bored in a relationship can lead to an unhealthy period of your life. But if you are putting in the effort, you know that boredom is far away from your relationship and you.

Have you ever wondered about what it would be like to be with someone else? Even when you are in a relationship. If you have, then that is a sign that you have fallen victim to boredom. It is natural for a person to find more than one person attractive but always pay attention to what is the factor that is causing you to daydream about someone else, and it is simply because you are bored with your relationship. Because if that is the case, you need to make your relationship more exciting or talk and discuss matters with your partner.

Many people in this world are happy to be single, as they say, to be free of any commitment but are that the case with you. Do you wish that you were single? Or envying the single status of your friends? If yes, then you need to take a closer look at your relationship; it may turn out that you feel bored with your relationship, that you no longer feel the passion and excitement of the earlier days of your relationship. If you are glad that your partner is busy with something else, then that is a sign that you are bored.

Don't let boredom be the end of your relationship; you can seek help from relationship counselors, or you can sit around and discuss these matters. Together you can always find a solution to every problem. All relationship requires efforts, so put in your step and let your relationship bloom.

.

Chapter 5:
Feeling Insecure In Your Relationship

No matter how perfect a relationship sounds or seems, there is always something that pushes you off on the opposing side. That is feeling insecure. This feeling of being insecure is what makes us doubt ourselves and our partners. A relationship needs to build around trust and feeling secure in it. When you lack those factors, it's only natural that you might fall now or then; it often happens when you feel like your needs are not getting fulfilled by your partner. You will eventually come to realize that you wanted something else. It also occurs when you keep all the problems to yourself, thus, not trusting each other enough to share. These problems then become your demise, and eventually, you are unable to take them. You realize that going separate ways is the only option when you need a good conversation about your problems and listening to what your partner has to say. Giving them a chance and solving your problems together is how you will strengthen your bond, and that's how you will overcome your fears, as we all know that trust is the foundation of any relationship.

It would be best if you let go of things. When you start a relationship with a person you care about, you learn to leave something behind. You watch movies that they like or eat the food they want. Sacrifice is a common ground you both walk on. You have to learn to go by their choices sometimes. But, the same should be done with you. They should do the same for you, if not more. You both need to make some compensations along the way of your relationship. You have to give each other choices. You have to trust each other enough to know that they might be doing the right thing for you or making the right choice for you.

So, the most common factor is trust. Many relationships have been broken because of a lack of confidence. Trust comes very handily when you need to go through a difficult phase of your life. You need the support of your partner, and you just need them by your side. That means trusting them to stay with you through your worst. Growing together is what you need to fulfill in a relationship. And sometimes, while doing so, we meet disappointment. Lack of trust drives you to get annoyed quickly, and you start to get distant. Growing apart may seem complicated, but you think it's better than stay together. These insecurities are very hard to overcome, and all you would need is time. But, know that it is your mind speaking most of the time. That is why taking a chance is such a considerable risk that we sometimes do not bother with it. We have to game risk to know if there is a spark between you two to keep all the light alive. Or if it is just a dead end.

It would be best if you gave yourself a lecture on positivity now and then. It would help if you got rid of all the evil thoughts that are driving you towards doubt. Gain more confidence in yourself and gain more confidence in your partner. Believe in each other. Try to stay positive in every situation. And believe in the best possible outcome of your situation in your relationship. Surround yourself with good thoughts and feelings. Always motivate your partner in the best way possible and think of them as your equal. Share everything, good or bad, with them. You will see getting rid of your insecurities slowly by taking these small measures towards your relationship.

You just need to overcome your differences by talking and listening. Both of you need a little break now and then. You need to give them space often, but not such that they start to believe you are ignoring them. You need to shower your attention and make sure that this whole relationship works out in your favor. Don't get jealous of their interaction with another gender, but trust them to be loyal to you. Give them love and receive love from them. Insecurities are often built on false rumors or accusations. It would help if you stopped a little to process every time. And just know that in this case, your partner's words matter greatly. Make it work out, and try to feel as secure as possible with them around you.

Chapter 6:
Dealing With Money In Relationships

When two people first get together, they don't know about each other's financial status. The way a person dresses can never tell how much money they have, as you might have seen people dress humbly but have quite a lot of money. On the other hand, some people spend their money on expensive items and clothes but, in reality, are not that rich. For many people, being financially stable is an essential factor in a relationship. As we have heard, many people say that when you love someone, truly money doesn't matter, but some people hold a different point of view.

However, it is entirely understandable that not everyone chooses love over money; for some people, money is a significant factor in life, but that doesn't mean that one should simply end things with their partner because of their low income. You can always encourage them and help them grow. Believing in your partner is an essential factor in every relationship; if your partner is trying to improve their financial status, then you should be there to give them the strength to continue their hard work.

One should always tell the truth about their income; lying will surely gain you some attention, but the person who truly loves you finds about your lie. It will be hard explaining it to them, and worse, it will end in an awkward situation. Money may attract attention, but in the end, the person who loves you will not be so happy with you, taking you for a lier they may end things. Hence, it is best always to be honest.

One should never date someone just because of their high income; you never know what that kind of person is like. Before starting a relationship, the best thing to do is to get to know each other because getting together with someone just because they are financially stable doesn't always end well. Getting together with someone just because of money can lead to a toxic relationship and may even turn into an abusive one. When you date someone for cash, your subconscious mind starts believing that your partner is the one in control, while in reality, both the partners have an equal role.

No one likes debt, but most of us have obligations. Sometimes, these debts are just a minor inconvenience, but other times, the burden is too much for a person to handle alone. So, always be honest about your financial situation, don't feel embarrassed; maybe when you share your case, your partner may also open about something. When you open up about your situation, you and your partner can find a solution together, and you can easily manage your debts and, with time, even get rid of them all.

When two people in a relationship decide to live together, it may be exciting at first, but the bills are always hard to pay. In such a case, you should always discuss these things with your partner about splitting the bill. Sometimes, you can't always divide the bill because your partner may not have told you but may be suffering from a few financial problems. So, it's better to discuss this kind of thing.

If things are coming to an end because of financial reasons, but you love each other and are willing to work it out, one should seek a relationship counselor. A relationship counselor is an expert at resolving such matters. The counselor can help resolve many problems, including debts, different spending habits, etc.

Always discuss your lifestyle choices if one of you has a costly taste, but your partner can't support it. That may become a problem; if such a problem occurs, then the best thing to do is to discuss such matters, as we all know a healthy relationship demands a person to compromise. Always remember that your relationship with this person is for a reason, so don't give up without trying, try to be honest, discuss things with your partner that is bothering you, and you would be well and good to go.

Chapter 7:
How To Deal With Feeling Anxious In A Relationship

How To Deal With Feeling Anxious In A Relationship

There are different ways in which relationship anxiety can show up. A lot of people, when they are forming a commitment or when they are in the early stages of their relationship, feel a little insecure now; this is not something we would consider unusual, so if you have doubts or fears, you don't need to worry if they are not affecting you a lot. But sometimes, what happens is that these doubts and anxious thoughts creep into your day-to-day life. We will list some of the signs of relationship anxiety so you can figure them out for yourself, and then we will tell you how to deal with them.

1. Wondering if you matter to your partner
2. Worrying they want to breakup
3. Doubting your partners feeling for you
4. Sabotaging the relationship

These are some of the signs of relationship anxiety; now, it can take time to get to the roots of what is causing this. Right now, we will tell you how you can overcome it; yes, you read that right, you can overcome it no matter how hard it feels like at the moment. However, it will take time and consistent effort. The first thing you should do is manage anxiety early as soon as you see the symptoms because you keep delaying it. It will become a problem for you. What will help you is maintaining your identity. When you and your partner start getting closer, you will shift the key parts of your identity to make room for your partner and the relationship. You need to know that this does not help either of you. You will lose yourself, and your partner will lose the person they fell in love with. Secondly, practice good communication. If there is something specific they are doing that is fueling your anxiety, whether it's not making their bed after they wakeup or spending a lot of time on their phone, talk to them about it and try to be non-accusatory and respective about also use I statement these can be a huge help during such conversations. If you feel like things are getting out of control and you will not handle them on your own, talk to a therapist that will get you some clarity. Because it's a relationship issue, try talking to a therapist that works with couples because that can be particularly helpful for you, so if you both have any underlying needs, the therapist will be able to communicate that in a better way.

Chapter 8:
Dealing With Abuse In A Relationship

Why can't they simply leave the relationship? This is one question that people frequently ask when they see someone is being abused in a relationship. But if you are the one who is in an abusive relationship, you will know that it not this easy. Ending a relationship that means a lot to you is never easy to end. It gets even more difficult when you have been psychologically beaten down, physically threatened, isolated from your friends and family, and financially controlled. If you are in an abusive relationship and want to leave, you might be feeling torn or confused—one moment you want to leave, the other you want to stay. You might even blame yourself for the abuse. If you are in an abusive relationship, we want you to remember;

- You are not to blame for being battered or mistreated.

- You deserve a safe and happy life.

- You are not the cause of your partner's abusive behavior.

- You are not alone. People are waiting to help.

- You deserve to be treated with respect.

- Your children deserve a safe and happy life.

Now, when you have to decide whether to stay in a relationship or to leave, here are some of the things you should keep in mind:

If you're hoping abusive partners will change, that is probably not going to happen; these people have deep psychological and emotional issues; although change is not something that is impossible but is not easy or quick, and change is only possible if the abuser takes full responsibility for their behavior.

Suppose you believe you can help your abuser. In that case, that is a natural phenomenon you will that you are the only one who understands them or that it is your responsibility to fix their problems. Still, the actual truth is that when you stay, you accept constant abuse, and you enable them, so instead of helping them, you are perpetuating the problem.

Suppose your partner has promised to stop the abuse. In that case, that is probably what they say at the moment because when they face, the consequences they plead for another chance and promise to change or beg for forgiveness. They might even mean it at the moment, but their actual goal is to stay in control and keep you from leaving them, and as soon as you will forgive them, they will return to their abusive behavior as soon as you forgive them because they are no longer worried that you will leave them.

Even If your partner is in counseling, there is no guarantee that they will change; there are many abusers that go through and continue to be violent, aggressive, controlling, and abusive. Suppose your partner has stopped making excuses and is showing visible signs of change, then that is good. However, you should decide based on who they are right now, not on the hope of who they would become.

If you are worried about what will happen once you leave, it is valid to be afraid of your abusive partner's will and where you will go, or how you will support your children or yourself. But you should not let this fear of the unknown keep you in an abusive relationship.

Here are some signs that your abuser is not changing

- They minimize the abuse or denies how serious it was.
- They pressurize you to make decisions about the relationship.
- They say that they can't change unless you stay with him and support him.
- You have to push him to stay in treatment.
- They tell you that you owe him another chance.
- They try to get sympathy from you, your children, or your family and friends.
- They claim that you're the abusive one.
- They pressure you to go to couple's counseling.
- They expect something from you in exchange for getting help.
- They continue to blame others for his behavior.

King of Hearts

PART 3

Chapter 1:
9 Tips On How To Have A Strong Relationship

9 Tips on How To Have A Strong Relationship

Who doesn't want a strong relationship? Everyone wants to have that high-level understanding with their partner that lasts a lifetime. It is scientifically proven that people who are in healthy relationships have less stress and more happiness.

Healthy relationship not only helps us increase our overall feelings of happiness, but stress-reduction also helps us improve our overall quality of physical and mental health that make every-day life more pleasing to go through. Relationships can be in the form of family, work, friendships, and also romantic ones. Depending on the area that matters the most to you at this very point in your life, you can choose to focus on that specific one until you feel you are ready to focus on the next.

If building powerful relationships is a priority of yours as it is mine, then stay with me till the end of this video because we will be discussing **9 Magical** Tips on How To Have A Strong Relationship with whoever you want. Let's Begin.

Number one

Listen to Each Other

This is the first and probably the most important thing that you might want to take note of. Just think, how many arguments have you had that went in the wrong direction just because no one was willing to simply just listen? In order to understand each other's point of view both parties must be willing to open up their ears instead of their mouths first. You need to have the stamina to listen to their side of the story before airing yours.

If you truly want a healthy relationship then the foundations starts with a good listening ear. To listen not only when the other party have problems in their lives, but also when they have a problem with you. Develop a good sense of compassion and empathy in the process.

Bitter thoughts, grudge-holding, and negativity toward the other person only serve to weaken your relationships, not strengthen them. So try to understand each other, let the other person speak, and then sort things out in the best possible way.

Number two

Give Time For The Relationship To Grow

For any relationship to truly blossom, it is important to spend the necessary quality time together. Whether the relationship is with family members, friends, or lovers, it takes energy and effort nonetheless. Any amount of energy you spend on that person will reap its benefits later.

Now, I am not saying to drastically change your life or to go on adventures or expensive dates to make your relationship healthy. All you have to do is simply get yourself free for a day or night once a week and do something different together, like having a date night, playing games, cooking and eating, watching movies or whatever you like, just give your best at that time. Be present with them and don't be distracted checking your phone or replying work messages.

Number three
Give Time To Yourself

Now I needed to talk about this one right after the number two. I think a good relationship should be balanced. In the previous point, I talked about spending quality time in relationships, but I also don't mean that you should give all your energy to them or stop doing things that energizes your soul. Don't sacrifice your own hobbies for the sake of others. I agree that you need to take more initiative in relationships but at the same time you need to take care of your own happiness too. So give time to yourself and spend it doing things that fills your soul with happiness and gratefulness. You will feel recharged and fresh as a result when you engage in your relationships.

Number four
Learn To Appreciate Little Things

This point will touch more on the romantic relationship side of things. If you are in a relationship for quite a while then there is a chance that you might get complacent and too comfortable. You might also gradually forget the little things that make the person special. As a result the other person could potentially feel like you may be taking them for granted. To avoid this, you need to start making it a constant reminder to yourself to appreciate the little things your partner does for you. Say "I love you" to them, give cute little gifts, give them surprises and tell them how much they mean to you. You need to show your partner how much you love them so they never feel taken for granted. So yeah, start doing all this and make your bond strong!!

Number five
Learn To Forgive

It is well said, "relationships require a lot of forgiveness". As I mentioned earlier, bitter thoughts and grudge-holding just hurt your relationship in the long run. So if you want a happy relationship then you should learn to forgive. If there is something on your mind that your partner did and you can't forget then sit and talk to them about it and try to come up with a good solution. If any of you makes any mistake, you should forgive them with a smiling face and tell them that these little mistakes can't lessen your love. Work on yourself, make your heart ready for what you see coming and even what you don't see coming, and let things go in the right direction. You need to make your heart learn to forgive, this is the only key.

Number Six
Don't expect your partner to complete you

You should be confident about whatever you have. If you are looking for a healthy relationship then you should not expect your partner to complete you. Sometimes, we expect things from our partners which we lack and it can put a strain on your relationship. What you could do instead is to constantly work on yourself to the point that you feel you truly and rightfully deserving of every good thing that comes your way. That you feel secure and independent at the same time in the relationship. Loving yourself first goes a long way in maintaining a strong and healthy relationship with others.

Number Seven
Ways Of Showing Love

Different people show and receive love in their own unique ways. Understanding how the other party expresses or receives love is the key to building a strong relationship. Some people do it by caring for you while others express it through physical affection like hugs and kisses. If you don't know that the specific love language is between you and the other party then it might cause problems in the long run. To really ensure the other party feels loved you have to express it in the way that they receive the most strongly. Go find out what they are by asking them and then start giving it right away!

Number eight
Be Flexible

If you want a healthy relationship then you have to learn to be flexible as well. Flexible in the face of any changes that might occur in your relationship. It is a known fact that change is the only constant in life. We may never be prepared but we should do our best to adapt to new situations that we may find ourselves in. It is also therefore unrealistic not to expect our relationships to change as time progresses as well. Learn to adapt and grow in this new stage and you will be all the more happier for it.

Number nine
Make Decisions Jointly

A good and healthy relationship requires listening to each others' desires and concerns. While you may not always love to do the things that the other party wants, you should always try to find a compromise that suits both of your needs. Instead of insisting and making decisions all the time, try making decisions together that both of you will find enjoyable. Be it where to hang out, what to eat for a meal, where to go on a trip together, or even what kinds of products to buy for your home, make sure that the other party's points of view is heard so that they don't end up resenting you over the long run.

So that's it, guys, we are done with our today's topic of 9 Tips on How To Have A Strong Relationship. Now, it's time for you to share your thoughts. What do you think about these tips? Have you already tried them and do they work? And if you know some

other tips to make relationships strong then share them in the comment box to help others. If you got value then smash the like button and don't forget to subscribe to our channel as we will be talking about some amazing topics in the future. See you soon!

Chapter 2:
10 More Signs You Aren't Ready For A Relationship

Relationships can be complicated sometimes, but what makes them more complicated is we ourselves. There are times when we fail to understand when to step back and think in a different way about life. We often fail to understand where we stand and where the relationship should stand leading to a lot of anxiety and pain in the long run. Sometimes it's more important to step out of the flow and give yourself time to think about things deeper.

Here are 10 signs that show you might not be ready for a relationship just yet at this very moment:

1. When you aren't happy with your own self.

We often feel a relationship or another person can make us happy, but unfortunately, unless you are happy with your own self, no one can come and make you happy. As the saying goes, happiness is within. It is very important to first find what makes you happy in life and gives you freedom. Because unless we know how to make ourselves happy, we cannot be at peace with another person too.

2. When you feel a relationship will help you overcome your loneliness.

We all do get lonely sometimes. But a relationship isn't the solution for overcoming that. When we expect another person to help us get past the loneliness it just creates a lot of pressure on the other person and might end up suffocating them too. Read a good book, make some nice dinner, watch that favorite rom-com alone, get that pet which you always wanted, because you need to be your best friend first and when you know how to overcome your loneliness, the other person will love your company too.

3. When you aren't sure about the person and jumped into the relationship faster than you wanted to.

As much as it is important for someone to understand themselves, it is also very important for us to know the person we are planning on getting in a relationship with. Do you see that person with you 10 years down the lane? Is he the one you had dreamt your life with? A relationship is a two-way street. It is very important to express and set your standards and expectations in the relationship clear.

4. When you still aren't healed from your past.

We all have a past. Some memories are good some still give us nightmares, but it is very important to consider it as just a life lesson and move on. The more we stick to our past, the more distant we get from our future dreams and goals. If you keep thinking about how your ex broke the promises and cheated on you, you won't be able to see the good intentions of the current person who probably could have been there in the future too, but you couldn't be completely happy with them based on your past instincts.

5. When you have fear of commitments and the idea of making sacrifices pushes you away.

We all have fears inside of us. Fear of how things will turn out in the future, we get apprehensive of taking a serious step in life. Commitment should be given only when you are ready from inside because for any relationship to work out both of you should be on the same page and only when your heart tells you are ready!

6. When you have a lot of insecurities and self-doubts.

No one likes to stay with a person who is full of self-doubts and always needs validation for everything in life. You need to be confident about your own self first because only then you can grow in the relationship and motivate the other person to grow too. Too many insecurities come in when there is not enough communication and when you cannot openly express your fears to the person.

7. When the relationship is not motivating you to grow into a better version of yourself and boosting your personal growth.

If you find yourself in a relationship where your personal life and growth are stagnant, then you are with the wrong person. As much as you should be investing in the other person it is also very important to invest in yourself and help the other person invest in themselves too. If the relationship doesn't motivate you to achieve that dream, get that dream house one day, travel together to the favorite destination, have that dream cruise, and get the dream car together, then you might as well feel the need to rethink why is it so.

8. When you feel situations are one-sided in the relationship.

Sometimes we end up with people who are not as much into us as we are into them. Their efforts and actions don't match their words. So it is very important to be vocal about your expectations in the relationship and not stay in one just for the sake of being in a relationship. Along with love, understanding the sentiments, emotions, and vulnerabilities of a person is also very important and if the person is not matching up to the mark, life is too short to give chances to a person who won't care as much as you would.

9. When you get hindered in communicating openly.

Open communication is very important for a healthy relationship. If you are having inhibitions about talking about your problems and insecurities to the person, either because you feel they won't understand you or because any discussion with the person ends up in an argument, then quite understandably you are with the wrong person and need to get yourself out of the relationship.

10. Peer pressure and wrong decisions.

This happens for marriages too. Any kind of relationship should not happen under pressure. If it's because all your friends are engaged and/or committed to someone, doesn't necessarily mean you have to do the same. There are many more things to experience in life. Unless you really want to get along with someone, you shouldn't go in it just because you feel cornered and lonely among your friends. Make better choices and better stories to tell them and make them feel jealous of your single but happy life! ;)

So That's It For Today's Video. If you found this helpful, don't forget to like, subscribe, comment, and share this with someone important to you. I hope you learned something valuable today. Take care, have a good rest, and till the next video ☺

Chapter 3:
9 Signs Of A Toxic Relationship

Before getting into the video, let's talk about what's a toxic relationship? Dr. Lillian Glass, a California-based psychology expert defines the toxic relationship as "any relationship [between two people who] don't support each other, where there's conflict and one seeks to undermine the other, where there's competition, where there's disrespect and a lack of cohesiveness."

Signs of toxic relationships are all around us. The question is how do we know if we have one? And what are the exact signs of such a relationship? In this video, I'm going to tell you 9 main signs of a toxic relationship. So let's get right into it.

Main

1. Unhealthy Communication Patterns

Passive aggressiveness, aggressive or bullying styles of conversations that your partner engages with you could be a clear sign that something isn't right between the two of you. The relationship can turn toxic very quickly when either partner feels guilted into responding in a submissive way to please the other. Furthermore bad communication can also lead to avoiding talking to your partner. Instead of treating you with love and compassion, if your partner has animosity, criticism, sarcasm, and egoism in most of his conversations with you, then it can lead to hatred and thus poison the relationship. We all want a partner who can speak to us with kindness and understanding rather than someone who speaks to us in a threat-like manner.

2. Habits or Cycles of Cheating and lying

If you feel that your partner is cheating on you or lying to you, it will damage your trust in your partner and may also harm the relationship. Once trust is lost, it is very difficult to get it back. You may start to trust your partner in days or months, but the possibility always seems fragile. Relationships with distrust can turn good partners into jealous or suspicious people. Sometimes even your partner's unforgettable compromises can't repair trust if it is badly broken. So, if for some reason you can't trust your partner then the relationship is definitely toxic.

3. Your Loved Ones Strongly Disapproves of Your Partner

What people close to you think of your partner is one of the most important factors in determining whether the relationship is beneficial or one that could be toxic. So, make sure to pay close attention to what your friends, family, and loved ones are saying about your partner.

Your family and friends always want you to be safe and happy, so if they strongly dislike your partner then there must be a strong reason behind it. They may be able to see red flags in them that you might have otherwise overlooked that may point towards something toxic brewing. That reason or some hateful reactions of your loved ones against your partner can indicate that the relationship is not good for you.

4. Over-Dependency On Your Partner

It has been noted by several personality experts that those who are the least self-sufficient (but also most self-critical) tend to be the most toxic partners. Sometimes this is a symptom of an underlying relationship problem. Sometimes it is not. But when a partner is absent-minded or disinterested in "self-care", that can be a red flag.

5. Constant Fears of Being Judged

Signs of toxic relationships can also include the feeling like you are constantly being judged. You may wonder why you always feel like you need to be on your best behavior. Or, you may think that you always get in trouble with your partner. Some partners can even pick fights as a way of getting back at their relationship - and then some feel like nothing's ever going right.

6. Feeling like you are being taken advantage of

One of the most important signs of toxic relationship behavior is feeling like you're being exploited. You may feel like you're not really treated with care or value. Perhaps you question whether or not you are important enough. You may worry that your partner sees you as someone they can take for granted.

In fact, one of the core dynamics of toxic relationships is that the less valuable you feel, the less valuable your partner will feel. When you have a deep, internal belief that you are not significant, it can lead to behaviors that are meant to hurt you.

7. You Are Always Defending Your Partner

One classic sign of toxic relationship behavior is when you find yourself defending your partner against charges of hurting you or you feel guilty and always come first to apologize to your partner but you are not sure why.
When the lines of communication between you and your partner start to break down, you may find yourself defending your partner instead of talking to solve problems. When you and your partner argue, you may also hear your partner say things like "you just need to learn to get along with people," "your problem is with you, not with me" or "you just want to ruin my life." Such behavior is enough to call the relationship toxic.

8. All the compromise comes from you

Nobody can manage a good relationship with a partner if they are the only one doing all compromise, work, and love.
A good relationship can only be built with the cooperation of both life partners. However, if you do everything while your partner does nothing and never gives the relationship a better chance to improve, then, of course, the relationship is toxic to you.

9. Your Partner Suffers From Addictions

The use of drugs, especially alcohol or (maybe) cigarettes, has a devastating effect on all relationships and is a major reason for leaving relationships. If your partner is addicted to drugs, and you think you can't solve the problem then make sure to provide him/her medical help.
But if he/she is not ready at all to get rid of drugs and drinks too much alcohol regularly, you should consider the relationship toxic.

Closing

So that's it. We are done with our today's topic.

Remember that if you feel that you are in a toxic relationship, don't forget to seek help. Consult your friends and family, be open to their opinions and don't be afraid to end the relationship if it indeed turns out to be toxic. Remember that we only have one life to live and we deserve to be with a partner that can care and love us unconditionally in all the right ways.

Now it's your turn to share your thoughts. Do you know about any other signs of a toxic relationship? Let us know in the comments below. If you got value then hit the like and subscribe button.

Chapter 4:
10 Ways Men Fall In Love

Genuine and true Love is so rare that when you encounter it in any form, it's a beautiful thing to be utterly cherished in whatever form it takes. But how does one get this genuine and true Love? Almost every romantic movie, we have seen that a guy meets a girl and, sure enough, falls head over heels for her. But translating that into the real world can be quite a task. The science of attraction works wonders for us. Sometimes we are instantly drawn to some people. On the other hand, we couldn't care less for others. And quite a few times, things flow naturally in our direction, making it all feel surreal and causing butterflies.

A famous psychologist once said: "Love is about an expansion of the self whereby another person's interests, values, social network, and finances become part of your life just as you share your resources with them."

A human mind is, nonetheless, a very complex organ. It can either makes you feel like you're on top of the world with its positive attitude or under it with its negative one. And a male mind, perhaps, seems always like a mystery to us. But it's not such rocket science that we can't get our hands on it. If you're developing feelings for someone and need a bit of guidance to get the man of your dreams to notice you and care about you, then you've just come to the right place!

Here are some ways about what a man needs to fall in Love.

1. **Always Be Yourself:**

Keeping a façade of fake personality and pretending to be someone you're not can be a huge turn-off for men. Instead let the guy know the real you. Let them see who you really are and what you really have to offer. You will not only gain respect from them, but you wouldn't have to keep hiding behind a mask. If you're pretending to be someone else, that only suggests that you're not comfortable with yourself. And many guys will realize this shortcoming and quickly become disinterested. You don't have to dumb down your intellect or put a damper on your exuberant personality. Men like women who are completely honest with them from the start. Who shows them their vulnerable side as well as their opinionated and intelligent one. You're in no need to pretend that your IQ isn't off the charts. Be your genuine, miserable, confident, and independent self always. That way, he will know exactly what he's getting into.

2. **Make him feel accepted and appreciated:**

From a simple thank you text to calling him and asking him about his day, making small gestures for him, and complimenting and praising him, a man needs it all. Men don't always show it, but they are loved to be told that they look good, they're doing a good job, or how intellectual they are. Sometimes men are confused about where women may stand, and they want to see that he's being supported beyond any superficial matter. When men share glimpses of their inner self with you and put themselves in a vulnerable position, which men rarely do, this is when it's crucial to make him feel rest assured that he will be accepted and appreciated. If women make men feel lifted high and admired, then it's pure magic for them. His heart will make such a deep connection with you that it can only be amplified from thereon.

3. **Listen! Don't just talk:**
4.

You would see a lot of men complain that they are not heard enough. And quite frankly, it is true. It's essential to establish a mutual balance in the conversation. Women shouldn't make it all about themselves. They need to let the men speak and hear them attentively, and respond accordingly. Ask him questions about his life and his passion, his likes and dislikes. That way, he'll know that you are genuinely interested in him. Men have a lot to say when you show that you can listen. They'll be more inclined to say the things that matter.

5. **Laugh out loud with him:**

Men tend to make the women of their liking laugh a lot. When you're laughing, you're setting off chemicals in a guy's brain to feel good. Make him feel like he has a great sense of humor, and he's making you happy with his silly and jolly mannerism. Similarly, men are attracted to women who have a spirit that can make them feel good. Tell him enjoyable stories, roast people with him, jump in on his jokes and laugh wholeheartedly with him. He will become attracted to you.

6. Look your best:

You don't have to shred a few pounds, or get clear, glowing skin, or change your hairstyle to impress the men of your liking. You have to be confident enough in your skin! Men love a confident woman who feels secure about herself and her appearance. You don't even have to wear body-hugging clothes or tight jeans to make him drool over you (Of course, you can wear them if you want). But a simple pair of jeans and a t-shirt can go a long way too. Just remember to clean yourself up nice, put on nice simple clothes, wear that unique perfume, style up your hair a bit, and voila! You're good to go.

7. Be trustworthy:

Another reason that men instantly attract you is when they have the surety that they can trust you with anything and everything. According to love and marriage experts "Trust is not something all loving relationships start with, but successful marriages and relationships thrive on it. Trust is so pervasive that it becomes part of the fabric of these strong relationship." If you want to win a man's heart, reassure him that he can be vulnerable around you and make him feel accepted and secure.

8. **Don't try to change him:**

"He's completely right for me... if only he didn't dress up like that or snore during his sleep."
Sure we might have a few things on our list about how our partner should be, but that doesn't mean we should forcibly try to change their habits. He might have a few annoying habits that will get on your nerves now and then, but that shouldn't be a dealbreaker for you. Instead, we should accept him with all his wits and flaws. You shouldn't just tolerate his little quirks but rather try to admire them too. If something about him is bothering you, try talking to him politely about it. And he might consider changing it for you!

9. **Have intellectual conversations with him:**

There's nothing that a man finds sexier than women with opinion and intellect. Get his views on a news article, engage him in a heated debate about controversial topics, put your views out the front; even if they clash with his, especially if they conflict with his, he'd be more interested and intrigued about knowing your stance. Show your future partner that you can carry on an intelligent conversation with him anytime he likes.

10. **Be patient:**

I can't stress enough that patience is perhaps the most vital key to getting a guy to fall for you. It would be best if you gave him time to analyze and process his feelings for you. If you tend to rush him on the subject, you might end up disappointed. Even if you do lose your cool, don't let him know it. Just be patient and consistent, and don't come off as too clingy or needy. If you appear too desperate, it's going to turn him off of the relationship entirely.

11. **Let him know you're thinking of him:**

In the early days of dating, you might be hesitant to tell him that you're thinking of him. You love it when he texts you randomly, saying he's thinking about you, so why not reciprocate it? Invest your time, energy, and efforts in him. Leave him short, sweet notes, or text him in the middle of the day saying that he is on your mind or sending him a greeting card with a cute personal message. Don't overdo it by reminding him constantly if he does not respond. None of these screams' overboard' and are guaranteed to make him smile.

Conclusion:

I hope this article deconstructed and gave you some insights into what makes a man fall for a woman. As the saying goes, 'Men are from mars and women are from Venus and Venus is great, but surely, we need to know about the inner workings of mars too.' Just keep the above tips in mind, be consistent and commit to him considerably, and you're good to go! If you found this video helpful, don't forget to like, subscribe, comment, and share this with someone important to you. I hope you learned something valuable today. Take care, have a good rest, and till the next video ☺

Chapter 5:
9 Signs an Introvert Likes You

A lot of people out there are conscious to know about the tell-tale signs that reveal if an Introvert Likes You or not. You are probably unsure if someone you know has a secret crush on you and you are eager to find out so that you can reciprocate those feelings, or maybe you want to be find out - out of mere curiosity.

Well, I want to first say that because there are many different kinds of introverts, we may not be able to cover all aspects of it. Some introverts like to be alone in their own comfort zones while others like to hang out with their inner circle of close friends and relatives. But basically an introvert is generally shy and more reserved by nature. They are usually more quiet and may seem like they have built up a little wall around them in the initial meetings you have with them.

In today's video, we are going into 9 specific signs than an Introvert Likes You. Hopefully this will shed a brighter light on this topic and bring you some lightbulb moments. So without any further delay, let's get right into it.

Number one
They will Try to Open up

Introverts are shy creatures that look for soul connection like a meeting of minds. So when an introvert likes you, they will try to open up, they will try to share their thoughts and feelings with you. They will tell you about that one best day of their life and they will tell you how they feel about themselves asking you, do you feel the same way?

So if an introvert overshares with you then you can take it as a plus point as they don't tell these things just to anyone. They tell you these things because you are special to them and they want you to share your world of thoughts too.

Number two
They Know A Lot About You

You might be amazed at this one and might be thinking, how can an introvert know that much about me so quickly? Ahmm, never underestimate their researching skills, just saying. If an introvert likes you then they could potentially look you up on social media, they might check out your posts to get to know who you are as a person a little more. They do their own behind-the-scenes search because they may be too shy to ask you in person, or they might do so to feel that they feel like they may know more about you before committing to liking you.

So if they know these little details about you then there is a high chance that they do indeed like you.

Number three
They Will Be First To View Or Like Whatever You Post On Social Media

This one also comes under the previous point. If an introvert likes you, they might be the first to like your post on social media because they may be too shy to message you directly or tell you in person that they find you interesting. An introvert will leave breadcrumbs behind to show that they are interested in you. So yeah, you gotta check if they are doing it or not.

Number four
They Look At You More Than Usual People

If an introvert likes you then they will surely check you out. Whenever they come in front of you or if you are sitting in a group then that introvert will look at you like more than once, without making you feel uncomfortable. Yes! They have this talent. So if you catch them looking at you, then they are probably into you.

Number five
Laughing Nervously

If an Introvert likes you then they might shutter or blush in your presence as well as laugh nervously. They can also get tongue-tied while talking to you. Want to know the reason? Let me tell you. When an introvert talks to you, they are actually out of their comfort zone, so that's why they appear hyper-alert. They are putting themselves out there. Give them the space to be themselves if they appear to be acting this way.

Number six
Immediately Answer your Call Or They Call You

Introverts generally don't like taking calls. It would not be wrong to say that they let all calls go to the voicemail unless it's the call from their food delivery guy. So if an introvert picks up your calls or calls you to talk to you then they might be head over heels over you.

Number seven
Inviting You To Hangouts

Here, I would go back to the first point where I said, introverts don't share their private world with a normal person. Introverts don't go out much but still, they have some favorite places like a coffee shop, a park that makes them feel good, or a hiking trail. So if an introvert takes you to these kinds of places, it means they want to share some part of what makes them feel good.

Number eight
They Step Out Of Their Comfort Zone

This is the most that an introvert can do for you. Do you imagine how difficult it is to step out of your comfort zone? Not everyone can do it except for the person who likes you unconditionally. So if an Introvert likes you, they would love to go to parties, or in a music festival only if they know you would be there. They can stay up late at night just to talk to you and to spend some time with you.

Number nine

Writing "Love Messages"

Now, you might be thinking if a person writes us a love letter then it's an obvious thing that they like us, how is it a sign then? Let me tell you how. Actually, an introvert's love message is different from others. They write things like, hey, how are you? How's your day going? Now, these things are common for an extrovert, they can ask these things to anyone but for an introvert, these messages are like love letters. As you know, introverts don't like talking much face to face so they explain their feelings by writing you a letter or sending you a text.

And writing is the apple pie of introverts. In writing, they can explain how they feel about you without being deficient of words but they will not do it. Introverts!! So if you are getting this kind of message or letters from an introvert, then it's an obvious thing that they like you.

So that's it, guys, we are done with our today's topic of nine Signs an Introvert Likes You. Now, it's time for you to share your thoughts. What do you think about these signs? Have you got your answer yet or not? And if you are an introvert then let us know if there are some additional things to help others. If you got value from this video then smash the like button and don't forget to subscribe to our channel as we will be talking about some amazing topics in the future. See you soon!

Chapter 6:
8 Signs You Have Found Your Soulmate

8 Signs You Have Found Your Soulmate

"People think a soulmate is your perfect fit, and that's what everyone wants. But a true soulmate is a mirror, the person who shows you everything that is holding you back, the person who brings you to your attention so you can change your life." - Elizabeth Gilbert.

Legends say that even before you were born, the name of your spiritual half was determined. The two souls roam around the world to find their significant other. Whenever they find one another, they will unite, and their spirits would become one. But finding our long-lost soulmate isn't as easy as we think it is. Out of 7 billion people, it could take some time to find out our perfect match. However, when we meet them, we'll click with them instantly and just know in our hearts that they are made for us. A soulmate is someone you keep coming back to, no matter the struggles, challenges, obstacles, downfalls, or any of the circumstances. Everything would feel perfect with them. But how do you know if someone is your soulmate? You needn't worry! We have compiled for you below the signs that you may have found your soulmate.

1. They would bring the best in you:

Have your friends called you boring or a party pooper since you have entered adult life? Of course, you blame it all on the fact that you have grown up now and have responsibilities. But there's this one person who tends to bring out the fun and sassy side of yours. You feel so comfortable around them that you're even willing to try new things with them. They make your anxiety and fear go away in the blink of an eye. Be it singing songs loudly in the crowd, trying bungee jumping, or just packing up your bags and moving across the country with them to pursue your goals and dreams, they will strengthen you by supporting your decisions and being there for you.

2. They won't play games with you:

They won't be inconsistent with you, like making you feel special one day and ignoring you completely the next. You won't be questioning his feelings about you or putting yourself in a state of over-thinking. Sure, they won't make grand gestures like showing up at your window holding a guitar at 3 in the morning or putting up a billboard saying how much they love you (although we will happily accept both). Still, they will make you realize your worth in their life by always prioritizing you, making you happy, asking about you throughout the day, and paying close attention to whatever you say.

3. You respect each other's differences:

When starting a new relationship, people tend to avoid or hold back specific thoughts, beliefs, or opinions. This is because, in the game of love, both of the couple's emotions are at stake. They don't speak their mind until and unless they're entirely comfortable with their partner. Your soulmate would always be open to change and respect your opinions and views, even if they disagree. They wouldn't ever implement their beliefs and ideas on you but would instead find comfort in knowing that you both don't have the same set of minds. It's essential to be on the same page with your partner on certain things, like the future, life goals, children, etc., but it's okay to have different moral and political views, as long as you both respect each other and it doesn't hurt the other's sentiments.

4. You forgive each other:

Being soulmates doesn't save you from the wrath of arguments and fights. Every relationship experiences indifference and frustration from time to time. But it is one of the things that makes your bond stronger with your partner. You both would rather sit and try to talk it through or sort it out instead of going to bed angry at each other. And when it comes to forgiving the other, you both would do it in a heartbeat. You wouldn't consider holding the other person guilty and would make unique gestures to try and make it up with them.

5. You give each other space:

Your partner doesn't constantly bug you by texting and calling you every minute. They don't ask you about your whereabouts and don't act overly possessive. And rightly so, you do the same with them. You give each other your space and know that the other person would always be there for you. Even if you have to ask them about some distance, they respect it without complaining. You both trust each other with your whole heart and respect them enough to give them the space they have asked for.

6. You empathize with each other:

If your soulmate tells you about them getting good grades in college, finding their dream job, or getting a promotion, you find yourself being more excited and happier for them than they are. Sometimes, we feel drained out by showing too much empathy to other people and understanding and friendly. But with your soulmate, you don't have to force it out or pretend, and it just comes naturally. Whenever they feel scared or anxious, you're right there with them, protecting them from the world and not leaving their side until you make sure they're okay.

7. You communicate with each other effectively:

They say that communication is essential for any long-lasting relationship. If you aren't communicating well with your partner, you might find yourself in the depths of overthinking the worst-case scenarios. Your partner makes it easy for you to share with them, even if you hadn't done the deed before. You find yourself talking about the tough things, the things that bother you or hurt you, and they comfort and console you reassure you that they will fix it. Similarly, you make sure your partner speaks your mind to you, and you do your best to right your wrongs and clear any of their doubts.

8. **You have seen each other's flaws and still loves each other the same:**

It isn't easy to accept someone with the habits or traits that you despise. However, you have been your complete and utter authentic version of yourself with them, and they still love you the same. Be it crying loudly while watching an emotional sitcom, binge eating at night, snoring, burping, or just showing them your weak and vulnerable phase when you tend to push everyone away and dress up like a homeless drug addict. They find your quirks cute and accept you with all your imperfections and flaws, and you do the same with them.

Conclusion:

A soulmate is someone who makes you realize your worth and brings out the best in you. They might drive you crazy, ignites your triggers, stirs your passions, but they might also be your most excellent teacher. They would allow you to discover your true self while always being there for you and supporting you all the way.

Chapter 7:
8 Signs A Girl Likes You

The human mind is considered one of the most complicated organs, and understanding the female mind can be a hell of a task. In 2017, a professor of neurobiology and behaviour, Larry Cahill, Ph.D., issued the differences between a male and a female mind in his research The Journal of neuroscience. He says that although the total brain size of men is more extensive than women, but a woman's hippocampus, critical to learning and memorization, is more significant than a man's and works differently. The two hemispheres of a woman's brain talk to each other more than a man's do.

Women are fascinating, inspiring, and quite complex creatures. And if you're unsure about the signs that a girl might like you, then you're in it for the long run. Mostly, men are expected to make the first move, like approaching a girl, striking up a conversation, or simply asking a girl out on a date. But women play the lead role in deciding whether a man can initiate romantic advances. They initiate the contact by subtly providing cues if the communication is welcome or not.

It's difficult to decipher a woman's behavior, especially if she's giving you mixed signals. But worry not! we're here to help you see the signs clearly of whether a girl likes you or not. So, save yourself some stress, put your decoder ring on, and let's get started.
Here are 8 signs to know if a girl likes you…

1. **She makes eye contact and holds it.**

While a lot of people shies away when making eye contact, if you see a girl holding it for more than a fraction of a second (3-5 seconds max), then there's a strong possibility that she's into you. Research says that when you see something that your brain likes, it releases oxytocin and dopamine into your system. These hormones make you feel incredibly joyous. Notice her eyes the next time she makes eye contact with you; if her pupils dilate, then she's definitely interested in you.

2. **She laughs at all your jokes (even the lame ones).**

When a woman notices a man she's interested in, she would smile, laugh, and giggle more often around him. Even if your jokes are terrible (everyone agrees), but this girl would act as if you're the funniest guy she's ever met. If she counterattacks you with the same humorous and playful banter instead of getting offended, then she's really interested in you. Relationship expert Kate Spring says humor is a sure-fire sign of confidence. And confidence sparks something deep inside women that sets off instant attraction.

3. **She mirrors your behavior.**

A study published in the Personality and Social Psychology Bulletin proved that subtle "behavioral mimicry" indicates that you're attracted to that person. You might notice that she has adopted your slang, the way that you move your hands while making a conversation, or the pace at which you talk. Jane McGonigal, researcher and author of The New York Times bestseller "Reality is Broken", calls mirroring a love detector. She says, "....the more we feel like we really understand somebody, we're really connecting with them, we're really really clicking with them, the more likely we are to mirror what they're doing physically."

4. **She makes frequent contact with you.**

Instigating conversations can be a lot of hard work for a woman since they expect the opposite gender to start the chit-chat. So, if she's constantly engaging in discussions with you, making efforts by replying to you properly, and getting to know you better, she certainly likes you. Relationship expert Dresean Ryan says, "Believe it or not, something as simple as a good morning text can show someone has deep feelings for you."

5. **She touches you.**

One of the most obvious signs that she's into you is when she touches you. It could be a light brush of her hand against yours, slapping your shoulder playfully, or touching your leg or hair. If she's initiating the touch and does not creep out by yours, instead she seems comfortable with you, then it's a great sign of her being interested in you. According to behavior analyst Jack Schafer, "women may lightly touch the arm of the person they are talking to. This light touch is not an invitation to a sexual encounter; it merely indicates that she likes you."

6. She gets nervous around you.

If you're around and she seems to become quiet all of a sudden or starts avoiding you, then know that she's nervous and not uninterested. She might start playing with her hair, rubbing her hands, interlacing her fingers, blink frequently, or compress her lips. If you also notice that her breathing has become ragged and fast when you've entered the room, then that's a lucky sign for you.

7. She's always available for you.

Whether you're in a middle of an existential crisis at 3 in the morning or simply want to go for lunch, you text her, and she's at your door the minute after. Even if she's busy, she'll move things around her schedule just to fit you in. You can easily tell by her body language and her behaviors that she loves spending time with you. She's always there for you whenever you need something, going through a bad phase, or enjoying life.

8. Her friends know about you.

Women tell their friends everything. And by everything, I mean every single thing. So, if she's confident enough to introduce you to her friends, then consider yourself lucky. If they tease her when you're around or start praising her more in front of you, then there's definitely more to the matter. The approval of family and friends is the most critical aspect in seeing whether the individual cares enough to see a future with you.

Conclusion:

Figuring out if a woman likes you is a very tricky business. You might get silences or mixed signals in the initial few days. But it would be best if you looked for the social cues that women give off when they're attracted to you. Try your best and do not give up, you'll eventually get her!

www.ingramcontent.com/pod-product-compliance
Lightning Source LLC
Chambersburg PA
CBHW071741080526
44588CB00013B/2110